Moving to/from Hawaii: Military Style

Written By

KC Atkins

Front Cover Photo taken on a beach toward North Shore in 2012
By
KC Atkins

Prologue

So you're moving to paradise? Ah, it is a great move that you will never forget. Congratulations! You might even decide to retire there. You just never know. There is one thing for certain, if you are a military family or a person/group that will be moving back to the mainland in a few years, there are a few things you should know.

Whether you are a single person or a family of 6, this book will work for you because it covers many basic facts. Please keep in mind though that the author and our friends are families – either with no children or with six children.

All of the points in this book are learned through my own experience and that of my friends in the military as we traveled to and from Hawaii. We have moved as recently as 2014. This is by no means an "end all" book but I certainly wish someone had told us these things BEFORE we got there. It would have made our transition so much BETTER. Some things are funny or horrible but it all is true. Good luck and enjoy your time on the islands – it will pass way too quickly. ALOHA!

Chapter One: Household Goods

Household Goods seems so odd to begin with but really it isn't all that odd. You need time to sell, sell, sell!

Is there anything that you couldn't live without in a house fire? That is what should be taken with you to Hawaii - even if you have small children. Take your important documents, pictures, jewelry and clothing. Anything else is just stuff. Stuff that will likely get tossed or resold by the end of your move anyway, that is IF it makes it there in one piece.

Most of our stuff was broken, damaged or ruined either going to or coming from Hawaii. That nice 60" flat screen TV with everything on it? Never made it on the truck. Coin collection? What coin collection? A tip with packers: When the guy comes and asks you if you want to declare anything and he's the one packing up all that stuff, make sure you declare it, because he is likely the guy that is going to the pawn shop after work to make a little extra on your move. The high school jewelry that you think isn't worth anything, declare it or take it with you, because when it is stolen from you, you will find it does mean something to you. All of the above actually happened.

Everything is not a horrible experience. This is worst-case scenario - but it does happen - a lot - especially when moving to the islands. These guys know that they will likely never see you again and that it will be months before you unpack your stuff. By then, they have moved on to other jobs or count on you not reporting them because too much time has passed. Protect yourself early on.

Do not count on the military paying for your damaged, lost or stolen items. This process needs a book of it's own. The point here is that it is a long process that must meet all the criteria, have strong documentation and be followed up on over and over – something that many people do not have a chance to do because of deployments, schools, work and various other obligations that come up.

Do not buy all new items when you arrive or get a new house. Why? Simple, most things do not wear out in 3 years (which is what most people are assigned at arrival) but not all people stay for the full 3 years. You may think why would anyone leave early? There are a ton of reasons, early retirement, promotion, a better position at a different post. You just can't count on the three years you go there with on your orders. We bought a new couch and ottoman to the tune of $1000 when we got there. It wasn't leather – big mistake because of the mold and it has been moved 4 times in less than 3 years to different houses and states. It seems impossible but if you have spent any time in the military, you know this is not only possible but highly probable.

So what do you do for furniture when you get there? Well, currently, there are a ton of Facebook resale groups that are on each base. I recommend beginning there. People are anxious to get rid of their stuff before they leave or want to buy something else and are willing to resale things a rock bottom prices. Additionally, many women do not have jobs and redecorate every year. Next, stop by the base thrift stores for various items. You would be surprised. I found a great pair of kids skis just before we left along with a snow suit. Funny. Although there is skiing on the big island – do not bring your equipment – rent it there. Likely, you will never ski on the big island. Finally, go local and try the local resale and thrift shops before going to the Naval Exchange at Pearl Harbor.

Recap of Household Goods Tips:

1. Get rid of as much furniture as possible before moving to OR when leaving Hawaii.
2. Do not count on the military reimbursing you for broken or stolen items. This will only happen if all your paperwork is correct, the sun is in alignment with Venus and your fourth child sleeps through the night. It happens but not always. Don't count on this.
3. Do not buy all new stuff upon arrival.
4. Buy used items beginning on the base where you live and then move outward.
5. Only buy retail prices after you have exhausted all other resources.

Chapter Two: Vehicles

It would be ideal to have the military ship your vehicles over for you, including that great jet boat or new Jeep but think twice before shipping vehicles. We have done this several times and it has NEVER worked out the way we thought it would. In Hawaii, this was especially true. Not only is there the possibility that your vehicle won't arrive when they say, because that happened. There is also the possibility that parts are jiggled while in transit. We had several different issues with vehicles both that were sent to and from Hawaii after we got them back. They were wear and tear items that would be hard to prove happened in transit. Things like: an oil leak that was never there before, a window lift that broke just a week or two after arrival or a sound that wasn't there before in the engine. One vehicle even blew up a few weeks after picking it up from the shippers back on mainland. Sure all of these things could have been coincidence but to have so many things happen like that to various people, it seems more like a shipping issue.

So what do you do? If you plan on taking a vehicle, take only one and plan to sell it before you leave. There are tons of vehicles available for sale there. It is not worth the hassle of shipping and registering your vehicle to take a 5-10+ year old car with you. A new car would be better off staying where it is but is more reasonable to take.

Again, buy used, on base first then move out from there.

Besides the shipping, your vehicle tags in almost every case HAVE TO BE REREGISTERED IN HAWAII WITHIN 30 DAYS OF ARRIVAL. Seriously. This is no joke. It doesn't matter that you updated your registration before you left, you will likely have to deal with this pleasant process right away. It is not as simple as going to the DMV. You have to get a note from the base DMO, get a safety check, get whatever needs to be fixed there taken care of, go back to the safety check place, go back to the base, then go to register your vehicle. It sounds simple and can be if you have all of your steps ordered out before you begin. Be careful to call about this procedure and do it in the proper order with the proper paperwork. If you don't, it will eat up even more of your time. If you have a large vehicle such as a truck with a lift kit or any sort of add on type items, you will have to go to the Recon (not to be confused with Special Forces Recon) lot in Waikiki for additional checks. It is most likely something that cannot be accomplished in a day.

Be sure to switch to Hawaiian insurance right when you get there as well, that is one of the items you will need to register. We had to drive across the island to get the official insurance card from our insurance. It cannot be a web copy or anything that isn't the official card from the company showing HAWAIIAN Insurance.

So you can see why I recommend buying from someone already on base, that has registered their vehicle on island.

Also, if your license is about to expire, get it renewed before you leave your state. If it expires in Hawaii, it can be another process to get that renewed as it will likely have to be switched to a Hawaii license. It all sounds easy but when you go through the process, you will see it is much better to call ahead, talk to someone that has done it AND check the website before you

Chapter Three: Pets

Pets are such an awesome part of our lives. They are important and should be lifetime partners. Unfortunately, in Hawaii, too many military families bring or purchase pets there only to leave them on island. Locals sometimes have a bad feeling towards military families because of this. One thing I would say is to really think long and hard about your decision regarding the animals. We did not take any to Hawaii but we did bring one back to mainland with us.

Getting your animal into Hawaii is difficult and can require many shots and kenneling during quarantine. There are no rabies on the island so they are extremely cautious with in coming animals.

There are no snakes on island and turtles and reptiles are very expensive to bring in. People still do it. The regulations change frequently. I would advise that you familiarize yourself before it gets too close to your departure date. Check with your local airline to begin with.

Another great resource: There is a great company that several of our friends used both going in and coming out of Hawaii: Island Pet Movers 808-783-8419. They loved the variety of options that this company offered. They are insightful.

Chapter Four: Documents

The best thing I can say here is that if you are a military family of any kind, you already know this but I will reiterate this: bring ALL your documents both to Hawaii and from Hawaii. It is not easy to get the kids medical records when you need to enroll them in school or sports or just the everyday activities on base when you don't have an address or you are an ocean away. That being said, there are a few things you need right away. Obviously, you will need all your vehicle documentation, the animal shots and documentation, Social Security Cards, Birth Certificates and immunization records for each person in your family.

Make sure that you have each document weeks before and then check again the week before, in case you took them out at one point and don't remember and then can't find them because everything is packed and you are missing the one crucial birth certificate for your son. It happens. I know. We almost missed our flight because of it. I had even checked several weeks before but had taken it out for something and it was in a purse that was packed. Thank goodness he had been born in the same city we were flying out of!

On some bases, just to get the children enrolled in the base activities you need shots, birth certificate and social security cards, along with a form from the activity and the fees. Additionally, you will need the name and number of 3 contact people ON THE ISLAND. I kid you not. There was no leeway on this one when we arrived on base.

ALWAYS CALL BEFORE YOU GO TO DO ANYTHING FOR THE FIRST TIME. If not, it is easy to become frustrated with things you thought would be easy. This makes paradise seem less like paradise and more like a pain in your bum. I took my daughter to enroll her in dance. She was 4. I took her on base and they were closed. Then they were open but the one person that could tell me about registration wasn't there. Then she was there, but I needed to take this form to a building I couldn't find and was closed when I did find it. I didn't have the right documents when they did open and then they needed my husband's signature and the numbers of 3 other people on the island for an emergency (I didn't know anyone on the island). Then I had to buy a card, take it back to the instructor, get her to sign my slip, go back to the other building and get my piece of paper saying we had paid and bring it back to the teacher, then my daughter could be in the class, that had just filled up while I was running around for a week trying to meet all the requirements. CALL FIRST! TALK TO SOMEONE. CHECK THE WEBSITE.

This all may seem like logic but when you get to Hawaii, things operate differently. Even the most basic tasks can be complicated by the many procedures in place that are not common on the main land.

Chapter Five: Money

You get COLA! This is extra pay to adjust for the higher cost of living in Hawaii. It is awesome. If you live on base, shop on base for most things and play your cards right by learning the cheapest way to enjoy all Hawaii has to offer, you can come away from Hawaii with some awesome memories and a pocketful of money.

When you get there, it can be tight. Most people spend at least 1-2 months in the hotels on base. There are some that are great and some that are literally a hotel room with a kitchenette. It can be tough. This is when it is easy to use the credit card and spend a bit when you first get there. Resist that urge. Do not eat fast food or at restaurants every night because you can. Buy at the commissary and prepare as best you can at your hotel.

Try to make sure you are wise with your money in Hawaii. There are a ton of free things to do. Spending money is not necessary. I would move back just for all the free outdoor activities available there.

Check out some of my suggestions in the EXTRAS! Section at the end of the book.

Chapter Six: Housing

I touched on this earlier. When you hear that there is a 2-month waiting list for houses, believe it. Plan for it. Do not think that you will be one of the lucky few that get a house early. You might just be that lucky one but it is better to prepare for the worst with the rest of the people than think you will get through.

First thing, even before you get there, get a mailbox at the UPS store and have your mail forwarded there. It is more private than trying to have it sent to the hotel. You may never see it if you have it sent to the hotel either.

Dealing with base housing is different on every base. The best thing I can tell you is to make friends with someone where you want to live and pick their brain on how they got there. Also, don't just sign up and never check back. Check back weekly or even more if you are so inclined. If you don't check back, you may be lost in the system. It is good to get to know the people that work there.

Do your research before you get there to see where you want to live, which housing areas have issues, which are the party houses, which are the younger groups and which are the family oriented groups.

If you have kids take them to the neighborhood park or events to get them involved. Talk to the others around you there. Your transition will go so much smoother if you have a friend or two to help you through. Almost everyone there loves to tell about thier move horrors and discoveries. You can learn a lot by listening to them.

Also, there are several places that you can live far from your base. Do not do this. Traffic can be bad both ways on the island and living way on the other side of the island can be very time consuming. In this case, it is much better to live where you work. I say that and that was the first time we lived on base. It was a pleasant experience overall – although a bit frustrating getting a house. I'm so glad we lived on base.

Chapter Seven: Schools vs. Homeschool

Homeschool or use that extra wad of cash that you were going to save sending your kids to private schools. Most of the schools are not up to the national public school standard. I would encourage you to check around your area. There are several schools that can be petitioned to attend but they are a drive that would have to be made daily.

Our children tried the base schools. We found that they were way below the level of learning that our children were at when we arrived. I ended up homeschooling until we left. There are groups that home school on the base. There are some great private schools around and if you are just set on the public school or base public school, I would suggest supplementing over the summer so that your children aren't too far behind when you leave Hawaii.

Another important topic for homeschool is supplies. In our previous duty station we purchased items at our local Dollar Store for a significant discount. Hawaii does not have any Dollar Stores – nothing that even compares. If you do need any of these items, either buy before you go, when you go home for vacation or pay a little more on the island.

Books for homeschool is also another topic. I found that being an Amazon Prime member helped tremendously when purchasing books or items of any sort. The shipping costs were nominal through Amazon.

That was our experience and my choice of homeschool.

Many of our children's friends went to the school on base with no problem. It was fun to watch them walk to school every morning. My friends enjoyed the traditional school choice and knew many more people and children than we did because of their interactions at the school level.

Chaper Eight: RELAX AND ENJOY!

After all the harried experiences and frustrating systems, I would still go back to Hawaii in a heartbeat. Why? Because it is a wonderful place if you know the system.

1. Call first.
2. Ask a friend or someone knowledgeable.
3. Check out the website.

Relax. Enjoy the island after you get settled in. Try to do one outdoor thing together with loved ones and/or new friends everyday or at least on the weekends.

People get island fever because they quit looking for things to do or ways to challenge themselves. You've done all the major hikes up Makapu or Diamond Head? Did you do the Pillboxes? How about the Pillboxes in half the time? Have you tried out all the shrimp trucks on the way to North Shore? How about turtle beach? Have you seen the turtles come in for their naps? Free fun is everywhere.

A ton of people suddenly take up photography or diving. ENJOY THE ISLANDS. Life is what you make of it there. Learn to enjoy the ALOHA. When you leave, do it all one more time before you go. You may think you won't miss it, but you will. I do and so do all of my friends that said they would never miss it.

Chapter Nine: Getting Plugged In

We were not like other couples that have to be surrounded by tons of friends every weekend. Our children were used to a certain group of military and non-military friends in our duty station prior to moving to Hawaii. With that in mind, I got the children enrolled in activities right away (the first week). That was one of the best decisions I made for their adjustment to the new environment.

When my husband left, it was immediately after the house hunting time ended. I was left on the island with no friends, no family, just me and the children. It wasn't a big deal since I had done many deployments and training cycles and been on my own for more than half of our 10 years of marriage. However, as time went on, I became involved in various groups around base. These friendships are ones that I cherish because we had an unusual experience of island life in common. I had never been big on getting involved in base activities but in this setting, I found the interaction to be rewarding.

One of the most valuable links I found was through the Women's Bible Study through the base chapel. While we only occasionally attended the base chapel, I found this group to be the most rewarding group I became a part of.

Many of my friends enjoyed MOPS (Mothers of Preschoolers) and the various book clubs on the base.

Another great place I found friends was at the local activities that we attended. My daughter took Taekwondo at a local studio and many of the parents and I clicked.

I even made friends with people I bought stuff from on Facebook. Finally, our neighbors became great friends. I was never a "neighbors are our friends" military spouse but in this case, neighbors were a great source of comfort because they were super nice people.

Facebook is currently a terrific resource. If you are on Facebook, search for your base, the news stations, the area around the base and the restaurants/stores that you think you might like. There are a lot of updates that you can find through Facebook.

Chapter Ten: Space Available on Military Flights

One of the best options that military personnel and families have is the option to ride Space Available on military flights. I would advise trying to use this if you have time to spare. This can be a great money saver.

We used space available travel several times. When my husband was in Okinawa, I took the kids to see him. It was fun and definitely something that the children will remember but expensive even with the free air fare.

I have to preface this with: I did a ton of research before I ever went to the airport. We were turned away 3 different days. When I finally got us on a flight, it was not the same flight I had been trying to get on and I did not realize that the flight over was not a direct flight. The gate agent did not mention this to me and it wasn't until we were seated on the aircraft that I realized that we would have an over night layover without a way to contact anyone. Awesome. A 1 year old, a 3 year old and me will be spending the night in a foreign country without my husband and no one to contact. The only thing I had going for me was that I felt safe as long as we were on base. I did not panic. I just tried to think things through on the long flight over.

The first thing we did upon arrival was board a bus (by this I mean we crammed into tiny minivans) and drive off base to get our passports stamped. Leaving the base was nerve racking. It was a confusing process that no one could really explain to me. After several hours we boarded a different bus (again tiny minivan) back to the airport, where everything was closed (including taxi service) and dark was approaching. I walked the 2 miles with a mountain of bags on the pushcart - that I am pretty sure is not supposed to leave the airport. My 3 year old was a trooper and my 1 year old was riding in a baby carrier on the front of me. Both children were tired and hungry.

We got to the base hotel where they told me they didn't have any rooms at first but somehow got me into a room in just enough time to order pizza from the on base delivery service right before they closed. It worked out and our children were terrific but if I wasn't a flexible person, it wouldn't have worked out. It was definitely an adventure.

I am telling you this so that when you try out Space Available, you will be flexible. The gate agents that we encountered were just that – gate agents. They are not in charge of the weather or the flight schedule. They can not help if the pilot decides they don't want to deal with passengers today. This is a privilege.

On the flight out of Okinawa, I was shocked at the treatment these gate agents endured. Many people were upset over being stuck for 9 days following a typhoon, including me. I never mistreated the gate agent. I saw many who did. Completely uncalled for. I was embarrassed for the people that acted like complete ingrates. I guarantee if people continue to act like they are entitled, the benefit will be taken away. So remember, be kind – every time you see that gate agent. They have a tough job and many did as much as they could to help people get home.

"Time to spare, travel by air." – Author unknown

I also took several flights between Hawaii and the mainland without much of a hitch. If you are traveling Space Available, please remember that it is not like a regular flight and can be a fun adventure if you are prepared to wait for several days if necessary. Keep your sense of humor and you will definitely have some funny stories for years to come.

Chapter Eleven: Time Off

What to do when you are all home? If you are off a long deployment, I would recommend enjoying the island the first time – if you haven't been able to do much because you have been working.

Once you feel that you have enjoyed the island, take that time to visit the different islands. There are a ton of ideas floating around out there. I would start with the Big Island and enjoy the volcanoes.

Everyone should try the following list of items at some point during their stay.

* Surfing
* Hiking – Diamond Head, Makapu Lighthouse and KoKo Head
* Shopping in Waikiki
* Pearl Harbor
* North Shore
* Turtle Beach/ Lanikea Beach
* Stopping for fresh coconut and sugar cane
* Pineapple Plantation
* Luau
* Aloha Stadium
* Hanuma Bay
* Snorkeling
* Diving
* Discovering the Hidden Island
* Exploring the various islands
* Checking out the volcanoes
* Skiing!!! How many people can say they skied in Hawaii?
* Explore Waikiki

EXTRAS!

A friend of mine is taking a trip this summer to Hawaii and asked me to put together some things to do on their two days in Oahu. I am sharing this with you as a bonus. These are some of our favorite brands and really fun things that we did over our 2 years there. This is not an exhaustive list but gives you an idea of what a typical day off from work can look like. I hope it helps you to begin to enjoy the island life.

From my email:

OAHU:

Best Coffee - We sent these to everyone one year for Christmas - they loved them!
http://www.lioncoffee.com/

Best place to shop for souvenirs (t-shirts, caps, Hawaiian shirts, etc):
Aloha Swap Meet at Aloha stadium on Oahu - near Pearl Harbor (open Weds and Sat 8-3 and Sun 6:30 - 3 $1 per person admission)
http://alohastadiumswapmeet.net/
Another good place is the International market place in Waikiki. But the cost is a little more.

Places to eat on Windward Side of Island (Other side from Honolulu):

North Shore - Cell service is spotty so be sure to look at all the websites before you get to North Shore

1) North Shore Burgers - good burgers - mid range price wise
http://www.northshoreburgers.com/ourstory.asp

2) Matsumoto's Snow Cones/Shaved Ice - seems weird but a taste of Hawaii for sure!
http://matsumotoshaveice.com/

3) Romi's Shrimp truck on the way - a little weird stopping for shrimp on the side of the road - but super yummy! Just trust me on this. You'll be glad you stopped. Have cash though. If I remember correctly it's cash only and their ATM breaks down a bit. If there is a line - it moves pretty quickly.
http://romyskahukuprawns.org/

4) Formaggio's in Kailua has a variety of food and is Superb. A little pricey but still good.
http://formaggio808.com/kailua/

5) Zippy's - good for donuts and a staple of island life. Cheap!
http://www.zippys.com/

Places to eat on Leeward side of Island (Honolulu)
1)Top of Waikiki - a rotating restaurant - a little pricey but fun and you can go in and just order appetizers and soup too.
http://topofwaikiki.com/

There are a ton of familiar places on this side of the island but I would challenge you to find some Hawaiian native restaurants or try something that is not a part of a mainland chain.

Pictures that PROVE (LOL) you've been to Hawaii!
1) You should find the Duke statute on Waikiki beach.

2) Something with the lush green mountains behind you and a little bit of the ocean.

3) Anything from North Shore - either shrimp truck or Matsumoto's from above.

4) Sea turtle - anything. They are my favorite animals to photograph.

Things to do

Most of our fun time was spent on the Windward side of the island. I would do the Pearl Harbor tour and Waikiki on one day and take the next day to go to the other side of the island. Both sides will be a bit crowded because it's summer but well worth the hassle.

Sample schedule would be as follows - doesn't really matter which one you do first:

Day One - Pearl Harbor/Souvenir Shopping

*Get up early and do the souvenir shopping at the Aloha stadium (opens at 8 AM on Sat and 6:30AM on Sun)
*Pearl Harbor tour
  http://pacifichistoricparks.org/phh_park_info.php
*Lunch somewhere there or near there - Ford Island if you can
*Waikiki in the afternoon or go to Paradise Cove Luau since already up that way
*If you don't do the luau - try dinner at the View of Waikiki
*Moonlit stroll on beach or pool side

Day Two - North Shore/Windward Side
MAKE SURE YOU HAVE A FULL TANK OF GAS BEFORE LEAVING HONOLULU AREA
*Get up early and head North on the H2- turn right on 83 (Kamehameha Highway) toward Hale'iwa/North SHore
*Stop at Matsumoto's for shaved ice
*Stop at one of the stands for fresh coconut - straight out of the coconut and try other native fruits
*Lanikea Beach (Turtle Beach - not to be confused with Turtle Bay - a resort) wait to see if the turtles come in for nap time on the beach - get feet wet here. Parking here is tricky - just stop along the side of the road. You'll see where everyone parks.
*Romy's shrimp truck - it's red and white with 2 ponds (now building) for lunch on way South bound 83
*Stop at Punalu'u beach
* If you need gas get it near the McDonald's otherwise it will be awhile before you see another gas station.
*Kailua - This is where Obama stays and is a bit of a ways down from here but the drive is nice. Some nice little boutiques across from Formaggio's.
*Makapu Lighthouse hike - super fun and a little challenging (1 1/2 hour walk)
http://hawaiistateparks.org/hiking/oahu/index.cfm?hike_id=23
*After the hike - Here is where you decide if you want to go on around the island or go back to Kailua for a great dinner at Formaggio's or continue around the South side of the island. Only do this if it is still light out - otherwise just go back using the H3 from Kailua. (Don't turn back toward North Shore - traffic is bad by this time and will take FOREVER to get back around - we made that mistake ONCE.)
*If you go South - there are breathtaking views and definite photo ops here. The cliffs are steep drop offs so only do this during the day unless you like to live on the edge. Look for the kite flyer guy off right after you leave Makapu Lighthouse area.
*Stop along turnouts for some great pics.

Optional Day
If you want to lay on the beach and snorkel –

Hanuma Bay is a great place for this but go early! Take some cash for the trolley up and down the hill. It's free entry for military but everyone needs their ID.
http://www.hanaumabay.info/
You could do that and then hike Diamond Head in the afternoon to dusk - to enjoy the gorgeous sunset.
http://www.hawaiistateparks.org/parks/oahu/index.cfm?park_id=15

Luaus on Oahu
Paradise Cove and Chief's are the two best luaus on the island. Get the better packages - it's worth it. Otherwise the food is cold. Discounted tickets are available at the ticket office on base. Reservations are usually necessary.
http://paradisecove.com/
http://www.chiefsluau.com/

<u>KONA:</u>
Awesome bakery on the Big Island:
http://www.bakeshophawaii.com/

www.ingramcontent.com/pod-product-compliance
Lightning Source LLC
Chambersburg PA
CBHW070258290526
45789CB00004B/1891